Cluisaz Bien

Very Best
Regards
Adele.

A Brenlots

Published by Olivier Troalen 2012

La Boheme
3 Mill Lane
Heatley
Lymm
Cheshire
WA13 9SD
www.laboheme.co.uk

ISBN No. 978-0-9574528-0-0

Design: www.jacksonhammond.co.uk
Photography: www.studio6photo.co.uk
Print: Hickling&Squires

Printed and bound in England 2012

Have a great time trying our recipes – bonne chance!

Dedicated to Louis and Nicolas

Kit de Cuisine Essentiel | Essential kitchen kit

With these kitchen basics, we will create taste sensations!

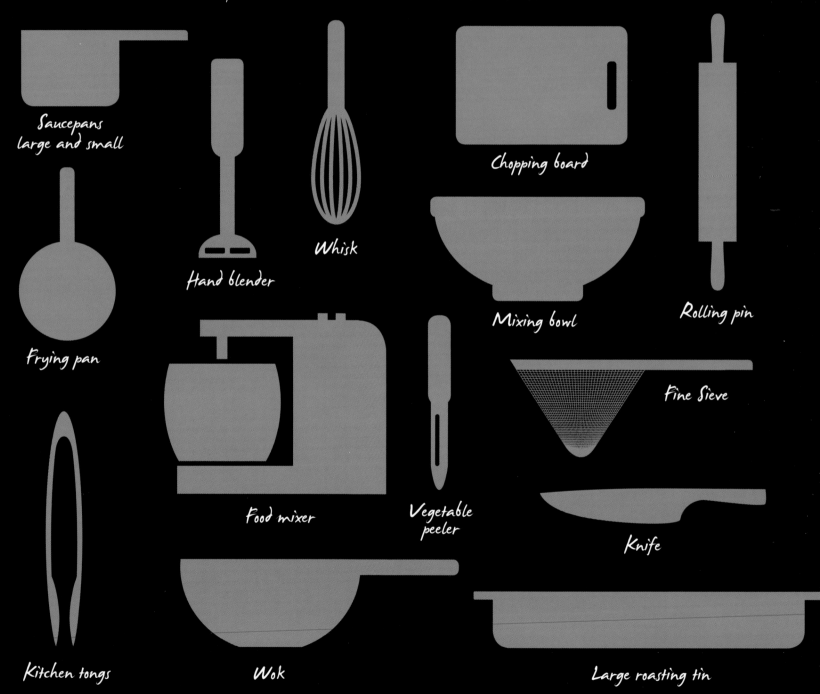

Saucepans large and small

Hand blender

Whisk

Chopping board

Rolling pin

Frying pan

Mixing bowl

Fine Sieve

Kitchen tongs

Food mixer

Vegetable peeler

Knife

Wok

Large roasting tin

Les Entrées | Starters

Sommaire | Contents

Page 22

Page 24

Page 28

Page 30

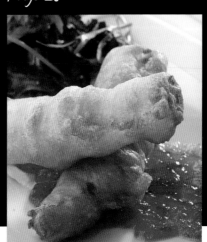

Les Plats | Mains

Page 46

Page 50

Page 56

Page 58

Les Desserts | Puds

Sommaire | Contents

Page 70

Page 74

Page 84

Page 68

This is me at age 5 training for the Tour de France

My mum, dad and uncles preparing that day's catch for the table

Les Premiers Jours | The Early Days

My wife Adele and I have been welcoming people to dine at "La Boheme" in Cheshire for the past twelve years, but the story of our popular, stylish restaurant – like so many good tales – began many years before when, in my youth, I decided to train as a waiter …

Always passionate about food and cooking, I trained at catering school in Paris before securing a position at the French Embassy in London during the 1990s. Mitterrand's Ambassador to England entertained the prominent politicians and socialites of the day: I had the good fortune to wait on Her Royal Highness, Queen Elizabeth II, Baroness Margaret Thatcher and Diana Princess of Wales when they all dined at the Embassy!

Leaving the world of political intrigue behind, I then moved to Manchester where I met Adele. It was whilst managing a restaurant in Chester, when my head chef had to leave due to family commitments, that I first tried to formally cook for customers. My appetite for cooking was truly cemented that night; I remember not only the adrenaline rush but also the sense of pure satisfaction and pride I experienced to this day. Resolving to leave management behind, and after ten years of fine-tuning my own cooking style, I was ready to pursue my true passion. It was time to look for suitable premises where, alongside Adele, I could make my dream of bringing decent French food cooked and served in elegant surroundings to the North West of England a reality.

The hand of fate intervened when La Boheme came on the market. As both Adele and I had worked there under previous

My first day at catering school with my family

'I like to think of myself as the conductor of a finely tuned orchestra – each member of the team has a role to play in ensuring the success of every service.'

Looking smart and ready to serve Royalty at the French Embassy!

management, we knew we had found the ideal place to achieve our vision of creating a unique dining experience where customers could enjoy good, honest French food in chic, relaxing surroundings. The only problem was timing! At this stage, we had two young children to look after, so the support of family and friends was desperately needed to allow us to commit with the necessary energy and passion to our dream. A cliché it may be, but it goes without saying to both sets of parents - Frank and Sheila, Pierre and Nadege - "We wouldn't be where we are without you." Even though purchasing La Boheme represented a huge risk, with trusted supporters such as Malcolm Gow and Richard Harding behind us from the outset, we persevered. And we are so glad we did!

Today, we hope that you think of La Boheme as we do: a place full of "joie de vivre" and somewhere each of you feel welcomed as a friend by dedicated staff whose attention to detail, commitment and service is truly appreciated.

Never one for following fashions or fads, I have dedicated myself to producing exciting, innovative and interesting food using local ingredients where possible. Delighted that our customers are open to having their palettes tested, I have consistently followed my own path in my menu selection over the years. I like to think of myself as the conductor of a finely tuned orchestra – each member of the team has a role to play in ensuring the success of every service. Thankfully, Didier and Alex have been with me all the way which is why I think so many of you return time after time to celebrate, commiserate, romance and even do business! I can now re-create that first adrenaline rush each time I look into my restaurant from the kitchen. I experience a genuine thrill hearing the buzz of conversation and laughter from the satisfied customers for whom we have cooked each and every night at La Boheme.

This recipe book represents another stage in the accomplishment we envisaged when we started La Boheme. Over the years, I have

My school mentors

Salmon fishing in Scotland with my Dad and Christophe

'If at first you don't succeed – have a glass of wine and try again!'

conducted many cookery demonstrations where, I hope, I have encouraged people to attempt my recipes at home. Often asked where my inspiration for the dishes I create comes from, my answer is always the same: from a flavour, a single ingredient or a previous dining experience. I feel extremely proud of the recipes in this book, representing as they do our customer favourites, requested by our regulars over the years as they share their life experiences with us in the restaurant.

Now in the Good Food Guide from customer recommendation and with your continued support, La Boheme continues to go from strength to strength. I hope you will try to recreate one of your own favourite dishes at home with these easy-to-follow instructions accompanied by my personal tips on each page.

And a final word: "If at first you don't succeed – have a glass of wine and try again!"

Bon Courage!

Olivier, Adele with sons Nicolas and Louis

We look forward to serving you with our finest food and wine. Adele and The Team La Boheme'

Les Entrées | Starters

Every great journey has
a first step and every
great meal has a starter.

Panier Basque
Chicken and chorizo filo basket

This is a great starter, with a great Spanish influence and full of flavour. This dish can be served as a main-course with some rice or pasta, and you can also add some scallops, king prawns or mussels.

If you can, try to find some small chorizos. They can be bought from a supermarket or butcher and they'll give a much better taste to the sauce.

Ingredients

2 to 3 chicken breasts
(cut into small strips)

250g butter

3 tbsp olive oil

1 shallot (finely chopped)

1 small chorizo sausage
(chopped)

1 small 1g packet of saffron

1 glass white wine

250ml whipping cream

1 glass orange juice

8 sun-dried tomatoes

4 spring onions (chopped)

2 avocados (chopped)

8 asparagus
(blanched then each cut into 3)

½ tbsp chicken stock *
(or ½ stock cube)

2 sheets filo pastry
(pre-bought)

50 to 100g butter (melted)

Method

Blanch the asparagus in salted boiling water for 1 minute (depending on their size; a little longer if they are thicker) then plunge them into iced water to help keep them nice and green. Undercook them slightly as they will need to cook a little more later. Have the spring onion chopped and cut the chicken breast into small strips and keep them in the fridge until needed.

To prepare the saffron sauce, pour a tablespoon of oil into a saucepan and gently sweat the chopped shallots and chopped chorizo. Add ⅓ packet of saffron and the white wine and reduce the sauce by ⅔, then add the orange juice and chicken stock and reduce by ½. Finally, add the cream and bring the sauce to the boil. Reduce the heat and continue to reduce the sauce until it becomes slightly thicker.

To make the filo pastry baskets, place 4 ramekins upside down on a thin oven tray and brush them with melted butter. Take 1 sheet of filo pastry and brush well with melted butter, cut into squares and place on the top of the ramekin. Repeat 3 times until each ramekin is well covered with layers of filo pastry. Place the tray of ramekins in a preheated oven 180C/350F/Gas 4 and cook for about 8 minutes until golden brown.

When cooked, take the pastry off the ramekins and keep them somewhere dry so they remain nice and fresh until needed.

Bring the saffron sauce back to the boil so that it is ready to add to the chicken.

To complete the dish, use a large frying pan so that all the ingredients cook quickly and don't get overcooked and dry. Add the oil and butter to your heated pan and add the chicken strips and season with salt and pepper. Pan fry quickly, cook the chicken strips to a golden colour, add the saffron sauce and just before serving, add the asparagus, avocado, sun-dried tomatoes and chopped spring onions.

To serve, place the prepared filo basket into the middle of a plate and gently spoon the chicken and sauce into the basket. Be careful not to overfill, as this will spoil the presentation. You can place a piece of flat parsley on the top for decoration.

Vive L' Espagne!

*I use Essential Cuisine stock, available to purchase online at www.essentialcuisine.com/homechef or at reputable farm shops and delis, see page 88

Soupe De Tomates Rôties Et Echalottes

Roasted tomato soup and shallots

I know you might be thinking, 'why do I need to make tomato soup when it is so freely available in any food shop?' Well, I'll tell you why: it's because you cannot beat a nice fresh tomato soup made from juicy ripe tomatoes. The texture and the taste is heavenly.

I guarantee that this soup will bring you applause from your guests. But to achieve it, you need perfect ripe plum tomatoes - if you find them still on the vine that's perfect. Serve this soup with some lovely olive bread or ciabatta and I will be a very happy French man.

Ingredients

4 large shallots
(around 400g weight)

12 large ripe tomatoes or
plum tomatoes 1.8 kg

5 tbsp or 50ml extra olive oil

¾ tbsp sea salt

½ tbsp cracked pepper

¾ tbsp granulated sugar

1 ltr chicken stock or
vegetable stock*

½ ltr good quality tomato juice

100ml double cream

2 tbsp tomato purée

6 tbsp basil pesto (optional)

Method

To make the soup, preheat the oven at 240C/475F/Gas 9. Cut the tomatoes into quarters, and peel and cut the shallots in half. Place them in a large roasting tray and drizzle with extra virgin olive oil.

Roast the tomatoes for about 30 minutes until they become coloured, add the sugar and roast them for another 10 minutes.

Transfer them to a large saucepan, add the chicken or vegetable stock and the tomato juice and tomato purée and bring the soup to the boil. Turn the heat to low and cook for a further 20 minutes.

Blend the soup carefully with a hand blender and pass it through a fine sieve. Check the seasoning, add the sugar, the vinegar and a little water if the soup is too thick, and reserve until needed.

To serve, reheat the soup on a low heat and at the last moment, add a drizzle of double cream and basil pesto.

Place the soup in the middle of the table and get stuck in with a piece of bread.

Et voilà!

*I use Essential Cuisine stock, available to purchase online at www.essentialcuisine.com/homechef or at reputable farm shops and delis, see page 88

Coquille St Jacques A Ma Façon

King scallops with sweet potato purée and wild mushrooms

I can't prepare a menu without fresh scallops, they are so sweet and tasty. This is a dish I created a few months ago. I love the creamy smooth sweet potato with a little kick of horseradish and the crispy bacon scallops. I feel this is a combination that works very well and I hope you like it.

Ingredients

12 large fresh king scallops

12 slices streaky bacon
(or 12 slices of Parma ham)

Olive oil

300g wild mushrooms

75g butter

Salt and pepper

Sweet potato purée

1 large sweet potato

50/100ml olive oil

2 tsp horseradish

Lemon thyme jus

3 bunches lemon thyme

10 chicken wings
(or 1 chicken carcass)

1 ltr water king scallops

1 tsp tomato purée

Chopped vegetables carrot, leek, celery

Parmesan tuiles (optional)

100g finely grated Parmesan

Method

Place the chicken, vegetables and tomato purée in a roasting tray with a dash of cooking oil. Roast in a preheated oven 200C/400F/Gas 6 for at least 30 minutes until the chicken and vegetables colour slightly. Transfer the bones and vegetables into a large pan, add the thyme and cover with cold water. Pour a little water into the roasting tray to collect the meat sugar and add it to the stock.

Reduce by ⅔ over a low heat then pass the stock through a fine sieve. Transfer the liquid into a small pan and reduce until very syrupy. Season to taste and add more fresh chopped thyme if required, reserve until needed.

With the help of the back of a knife, make the streaky bacon as thin as possible. Place one fresh king scallop on the piece of bacon and roll the bacon around it. Repeat the operation until all the scallops are covered. Place them in the fridge until needed.

To make the Parmesan tuiles, line a flat thin roasting tray with greaseproof paper and layer thinly with grated Parmesan. Cook in a preheated oven 180C/350F/Gas 4 for about 2 to 3 minutes until golden brown and reserve until needed.

To make the sweet potato purée

Wrap the sweet potato in foil and place it in a preheated oven at 170C/325F/Gas3 and roast for 20 to 30 minutes until the potato is very soft in the middle. Let it cool down for 30 minutes and remove the skin. Place in a small container and add the olive oil and horseradish and blend with a hand blender until smooth (add more oil if needed) check seasoning and reserve until needed.

The mushrooms and scallops take about the same time to cook so heat two tablespoons of olive oil in two separate frying pans. Get a pan hot and cook the mushrooms for two minutes, add a knob of butter and season at the end. Heat a second pan and cook the scallops for about 1 minute each side. You are now ready to complete the dish.

To serve, take a dessert spoon of sweet potato purée on the plate and use the back of the spoon to splay the purée. Add the wild mushroom, place the scallops around the plate, drizzle the thyme jus around the plate and add the Parmesan tuile.

C'est fini et quelle assiette!

Serves 6

Duo De Porc Fondant De Poireaux
Pork belly with black pudding and cider jus

This is an interesting dish and very popular at the restaurant. You can replace the black pudding with fresh king scallops. There are plenty of ways to cook the pork belly. I like to cook it slowly in the oven for 2 to 2½ hours to release all the meat juices and I then make a fantastic sauce with it. I advise you to cook the pork belly a day in advance to give it chance to cool down fully and leave the cooking stock to cool down so you can remove all the fat from the top of the stock.

Ingredients

1 kg pork belly

4 slices black pudding

4 tbsp vegetable oil

3 leeks (cut length-ways)

1 white onion (finely chopped)

50g butter

4 tbsp white wine vinegar

200ml whipping cream

Salt and pepper

1 head celery

2 tbsp tomato purée

1 can cider

1½ ltr water

2 carrots

3 onions (chopped)

1 bunch fresh thyme

2 tbsp of vegetable oil and plain flour mixed together to make a paste

C'est terminé, worth all the effort.

Method

Place a large roasting tray over a medium heat and when hot, add the rough cut vegetables and brown them for about 10 minutes. Place the pork belly on top of the vegetables, season the skin well and rub a few drops of vegetable oil on the skin. Try to make sure the belly is not in contact with the roasting dish.

Place in the bottom of a preheated oven at 240C/475F/Gas 9 (not on a shelf) for 1¼ hours.

Pour about 1½ litres of warm water into the roasting tray - just enough to submerge all the vegetables - add the tomato purée and cook for about 5 more minutes. Cover the roasting tray completely with foil and reduce the oven heat to 200C/400F/Gas 6 and cook for about 1¼ hours.

Regularly check the level of water and make sure it remains at the same level.

After 1¼ hours, check if the pork is ready by passing a knife through it. If the knife appears to resist, give it another 15 minutes and check again. Repeat until the knife passes through easily. When the pork is ready, remove the foil, switch off the oven and leave it for another 15 minutes. Take it out of the oven and leave the tray in a cold room to cool down for 1 hour.

When cool, take the belly out of the tray, place on a flat plate and place another plate upside down on top with something heavy to press the pork

belly down. Put it in the fridge and leave it until needed. Pass the stock through a sieve and place it in the fridge also.

Next day
To make the sauce, pour the cider into a saucepan and reduce by ⅔, add the pork stock and reduce again by ⅔ until you are happy with the taste. Add the chopped thyme and some of the flour and oil paste to the boiling sauce until you are happy with the consistency, then reserve until needed.

To make the leek and onion compote, place the finely chopped onion with a dash of butter in a saucepan over a medium heat, do not brown the onion. After 5 minutes, add the washed leeks, pour in the white wine vinegar and reduce until most of the vinegar has gone. Add the cream and reduce by half, check the seasoning and reserve.

You are now ready to assemble the dish.

Preheat the oven to 200C/400F/Gas 6. Gently warm the leek compote and pork jus separately. Bring the pork belly out of fridge, cut into neat matchbox squares and place on a thin roasting tray skin down. Heat in the oven for 5 to 7 minutes depending on the thickness and during the last 2 minutes, add the sliced black pudding.

Place the leek compote in the middle of the plate, then a slice of black pudding and roasted pork belly on the top. Pour a little of the jus around the plate.

Rouleau De Canard
Duck spring rolls

This is a bit of Chinese or oriental taste in the restaurant. I love duck spring rolls so I made some with a bit of French in them and I think they work well. An article in a foody magazine said my duck spring rolls would take some beating and would not be out of place in the best restaurant in Chinatown. That was good enough for me.

Ingredients

4 duck legs

5 tbsp hoi sin

8 tbsp plum sauce

1 small bunch fresh coriander

1 small sweet potato

5 spring onions (chopped)

1 packet beansprouts

Salt and pepper

1 packet spring roll pastry

50g flour

Oriental dressing

4 tbsp tomato ketchup

1 tbsp honey

Juice 1 orange

1 tbsp soy sauce

2 tbsp sesame oil

2 tbsp balsamic vinegar

1 tbsp sesame seeds

1 small bunch coriander

Method

For this recipe I use duck legs. Place the duck legs in a deep frying pan and cover with cooking oil. Cook them on a low heat for about 1½ hours until the duck feels soft. Remove and allow them to cool for ½ hour. Alternatively you can buy a whole duck and cover in a deep frying pan with water, 1 orange, salt and pepper and gently simmer for about 1½ hours.

When the duck cools down, remove the meat from the bone with a fork and shred. Place the meat in a large bowl.

Wrap the sweet potato in foil and roast it in a preheated oven 170C/325F/Gas 3 for about ½ hour, until very soft (check it with a knife). Peel when cool and with a fork, mash and reserve for later.

Pan fry the beansprouts very quickly in a little drop of sesame oil and reserve.

Add ¼ hoi sin sauce, ¼ plum sauce, the spring onions, beansprouts, chopped coriander and part of the sweet potato mash to the duck and mix until it becomes a paste. Taste your mixture for seasoning and add more flavour if required.

Spring roll pastry

In a small container place the flour and add a little water to make a thick "glue". Use 1 sheet of spring roll pastry and add some of your duck mix in the middle. Brush all around with the flour glue and wrap the pastry around your mixture. Turn the corners and roll to form the spring roll.

I suggest you repeat this operation one more time to ensure your pastry does not pierce when cooking. During rolling, keep a damp cloth over the remaining pastry sheets to prevent them from drying out.

Oriental dressing

Place all the ingredients in a blender and blend for 1 minute. Check the taste for seasoning.

To serve, deep fry the duck spring rolls in very hot oil for 1 minute and place in a hot oven for another 3 minutes. Place them on a bed of dressed salad leaves or rocket salad and drizzle the oriental dressing around the plate.

Un délice oriental with a French je ne sais quoi.

Soupe De Panais Rôti Au Curry Et Miel
Curried honey roast parsnip soup

This is a great soup on a cold winter's day. It is very smooth and sweet, with a hint of curry.

Ingredients

1 kg parsnips (peeled)

1 tbsp mild curry powder

3 tbsp cooking oil

3 tbsp honey

40g butter

2 medium onions (chopped)

1 head of celery (chopped)

4 chicken carcasses (ask your butcher for some)

1½ ltr water or use 1 ltr of chicken stock made from cubes or powder* (If you can, it is always better to make your own stock, but stock cubes and powder are also ok)

500ml single cream

250ml double cream (optional)

Salt and pepper

Method

Preheat the oven 170C/325F/Gas 3.

In a roasting tray, place the rough cut parsnips, oil and curry powder and roast for about 12 minutes, mixing from time to time.

During the last 4 minutes cooking time, add the honey, mix well and continue to roast, making sure they do not burn.

In a large saucepan melt the butter and sweat the chopped onion and celery for about 5 minutes.

To make the chicken stock, place the chicken carcasses into a large pot and cover with 1½ litres of water and bring to the boil very slowly. Skim off any scum that forms and simmer for about 30 minutes. Pass through a fine sieve and reserve until needed.

Add the chicken stock and slowly bring to the boil. Add the roasted parsnips and cook on low heat for another 30 minutes.

Remove from the heat, liquidise and pass through a sieve.

Return back to the heat and add the single cream until the preferred consistency is achieved, season and serve.

I like to serve this soup with a dash of double cream on top and a lot of warm bread.

*I use Essential Cuisine stock, available to purchase online at www.essentialcuisine.com/homechef or at reputable farm shops and delis, see page 88

Beignet D'Haddock
Smoked haddock fritters with sweet chilli and ginger dressing

What can I say about this dish? This is the most popular dish I've ever had at the restaurant. It has been on my menu for about 15 years and people come back for it time and time again. The first time I had it was in a restaurant in Didsbury. I've changed it a bit to my liking and my customers have got the same taste as me. The only problem with the dish is you need a small deep fat fryer. I know nowadays, people are not keen on them, but it is a small price to pay to achieve food heaven!

To produce this dish you need to buy natural smoked haddock NOT the bright yellow smoked haddock. The natural one is slightly smoked and not as dry as the other one. You also need to use the bigger chillies. You can use as many as you like to make the sauce as red and green as possible. The smaller the chillies, the hotter they are, and the sauce will be hot too.

Listen out for the compliments from your guests.

Ingredients

Beignet

1 large fillet smoked haddock

1 lemon (for garnish)

Salad leaves for serving

Batter

250ml beer

150g self raising flour

1 pinch salt

Sweet ginger and chilli sauce

4 ginger stems

4 tbsp stem ginger syrup

3 large green chillies

3 large red chillies

Salt and pepper

Juice ½ lemon

4 tbsp olive oil

Method

20 minutes before serving, make the batter. To prepare it, mix the beer, salt and flour together until smooth. Add a drop of cold water if too thick or add a bit of flour if too thin and reserve until needed.

To prepare the fillet of haddock, starting from the tail, simply put a knife under the skin and follow it all the way down the fish. The skin will come away very easily and can be removed by hand if preferred. Cut the fish into finger strips (around 2 or 3 strips per person) and place in the fridge until needed.

For the sweet ginger and chilli sauce, cut the red chillies length ways and de-seed with the help of a teaspoon. Blend together with 2 stems of ginger, 2 tablespoons of stem ginger syrup, 2 tablespoons of olive oil and lemon juice to make a smooth dressing consistency. Add a dash of water if too thick or more chillies if required.

Repeat the procedure with the green chillies and keep the 2 chilli dressings in the fridge until needed. Make sure you wash your hands properly after handling the chillies.

To serve, spoon some of the chilli/ginger dressings onto the plates and arrange some dressed salad leaves and ½ lemon.

10 minutes before serving switch on the fryer to 200C/400F/Gas 6. Coat the strips of haddock evenly in the batter and with the help of kitchen tongues, individually place the coated strips of haddock into the fryer to cook for about 2 to 3 minutes until crispy and golden brown. Repeat the process as necessary (do not put too many strips of haddock in the fryer at one time, as they could stick together and the oil could cool down and the haddock will become soggy).

When cooked, place them on a flat tray lined with kitchen paper to absorb the excess oil. Arrange them on the top of the chilli dressing and serve straight away.

Gratin De Fruits De Mer
Seafood gratin

Brittany is the French Cornwall and a paradise for shellfish. I first cooked this dish when I was there on holiday with my family. It's a very easy dish to create and can be served as a starter or main course. You can add more seafood such as squid, crab meat and clams or you can use fish like salmon, monkfish or plaice.

The most important thing is to use fresh mussels and keep the mussel cooking liquor for the sauce base to help create a fantastic sweet flavoured jus.

Ingredients

1 kg fresh mussels

4 large king scallops or 200g queen scallops

8 king prawns tails (peeled)

2 leeks (chopped lengthways)

1 tbsp fresh dill (chopped)

1 glass white wine

250ml double cream

1 lemon

1 cup breadcrumbs

4 large scallop shell (ask your fishmonger to reserve them for you)

Method

Pour the white wine into a large saucepan and add the cleaned mussels. Place a lid on the pan and cook for about 5 minutes on a medium heat, stirring a couple of times until the mussels are open. Allow to cool for a few minutes, then remove the mussels from their shells and reserve for later. Pass the liquid through a fine sieve and transfer the jus into a clean saucepan.

Add the leeks and cream and reduce slowly for 5 minutes. When ready, add the juice of 1 lemon and the chopped fresh dill and keep the sauce warm. If the sauce becomes too thick, add a little water.

Pour all the seafood into the hot sauce for 1 minute then spoon into the empty scallop shells. Alternatively, equally divide all the raw seafood between the empty scallop shells and pour the hot sauce over.

Sprinkle a handful of breadcrumbs on the top of each seafood gratin and place in a preheated oven 200C/400F/Gas 6 and cook for about 3 to 5 minutes until the gratin becomes golden brown and starts to bubble.

Serve straight away with a wedge of lemon and warm bread (French bread of course).

A tossed rocket salad can also be added on the side.

Guaranteed to impress!

Serves 4

Tarte Aux Trois Saveurs
Tart of three flavours

This is a very interesting mix of flavours. The sweetness of the pear with the blue cheese and leeks works "parfaitement"! You can also replace the blue cheese with goat's cheese and spinach for the leeks; the combinations are endless.

I prefer to cook them in small individual tartlet tins. The tart should be cooked 15 minutes before serving so they are easier to take out of the case and the tart is nicer served warm. Just take them out before your guests arrive and leave them in the oven which will still be warm from cooking them (ensure that the oven has been switched off first).

Ingredients

Pastry

150g butter

300g plain flour

5g salt

70ml cold water

Tart filling

3 leeks finely cut and washed

1 small tin cooked pears (cubed)

100g blue cheese (crumbled)

4 whole eggs

300ml double cream

200ml balsamic vinegar

Rocket salad (for garnish)

50g butter

Method

To make the balsamic dressing, pour the syrup from the tinned pears and balsamic vinegar into a saucepan. Heat and reduce until very syrupy and put in the fridge to cool.

The pastry
You can buy shortcrust pastry or if you prefer you can make it. To make the pastry, sieve the flour with the salt, add the butter and use your fingertips to rub the butter into the flour until you have a mixture that resembles coarse breadcrumbs with no large lumps of butter remaining. Try to work quickly so that it does not become greasy. Using a knife, stir in just enough of the cold water to bind the dough together.

Wrap in cling film and relax in the fridge for 2 hours.

Butter 4 or 5 tartlet tins 10cm/4" in diameter, roll out the pastry, line the tins and cut off the excess. Place in the fridge for at least 20 minutes.

The tart filling
In a saucepan, heat the butter, add the leeks, a pinch of salt and pepper, and cook slowly for about 6 minutes until the leeks are very soft, then leave to cool.

Meanwhile, whisk together the cream and eggs, add the pears (cubed), blue cheese (crumbled) and the cooked leeks and season.

Preheat the oven to 180C/350F/Gas 4. To cook the tarts, spoon the mixture into the raw pastry cases and bake for about 20 minutes until just beginning to set. Remove from the oven and leave to rest for 10 minutes before removing from the tartlet tins.

To serve, place the warm tart in the middle of a plate with some rocket salad which has been lightly tossed in a French dressing.

Drizzle the sweet balsamic dressing around the plate and add some walnuts to garnish.

Great work, you should be pleased with yourself!

Crème D'Oignon, Thym Et Cidre
Cream of onion soup with thyme and cider

Did you know that in France, this soup is served on a regular basis, at 4 or 5 o'clock in the morning after a good night out? Apparently it helps to cure your hangover, although I'm not convinced!

This is my version and one of the most popular soups at the restaurant. I love French onion soup I but find it very difficult to recreate the lovely sweet taste of the onion. Mostly, this is due to the quality of the onions; sometimes they don't have enough sweetness to produce this simple but beautiful soup. My alternative creation is to use sweet cider to bring the sweetness to the chicken stock and cream for its smooth taste.

Ingredients

5 chicken carcasses
(ask your butcher)

1 head celery (chopped)

2 large bunches fresh thyme

4 large white onions

1 can 440ml sweet cider

500ml whipping cream

4 tbsp plain flour

4 dessert spoons vegetable oil

Mix the flour and oil together
to make a paste

5 dessert spoons olive oil

Method

To make the chicken stock, place the chicken carcasses, ½ of the thyme and celery into a large pot and cover the ingredients with 3 litres of cold water. Bring to the boil, skim off any scum that forms and simmer.

Keep the ingredients covered during cooking by topping up with water whenever necessary. You will need about 2 litres of chicken stock when finished.

After about 1 hour, season the stock to taste, then pass it through a sieve and ladle off any surplus fat. The stock can be made the day before and left in the fridge overnight, this makes removing the fat easier.

Peel the onions, cut them in half (husband's job), slice very thinly and cook them in a large saucepan with 5 dessert spoons of olive oil on a medium heat, put a lid on and cook slowly for about 30 minutes until they become very soft and slightly brown. (It's important not to let the onions burn, as the soup will become bitter and taste horrible.) Strip the thyme from the stem and add to the soft onion.

Add the cider and reduce by ⅓ then add the chicken stock and reduce by ⅓ again. You can continue to reduce until you are happy with the flavour. Pour the cream into the soup and bring back to the boil on a very low heat and cook for another 10 minutes.

Last, but so important, check the seasoning and consistency. If you feel the soup is a little bit runny, then gradually add the flour and oil paste to the boiling soup until it reaches a lovely consistency.

You can serve the soup as it is or you can blend it with a hand blender and pass it through a fine sieve. If you blend it, you may need to make the soup thicker again using the flour and oil paste.

Serve the soup with warm French baguette and butter. C'est délicieux!

Assiette De Chèvre Aux Poivrons Rôtis

Grilled goat's cheese with chilled roast pepper and tomato compote

This a very colourful and tasty dish, ideal for a light starter. It consists of chilled pepper, tomato compote, gratinated goat's cheese with honey and sesame seeds served on French toast and accompanied with a basil pesto dressing.

Ingredients

4 peppers
(different colours if possible)

1 small white onion (chopped)

6 tomatoes

1 tsp white wine vinegar

1 tsp tomato purée

4 small goat's cheeses

½ tsp granulated sugar

½ tsp ground cumin

2 tbsp clear honey

1 tbsp sesame seeds

2 small French sticks

Salt and pepper

Pesto dressing

250ml extra-virgin oil

1 large bunch fresh basil

1 tsp roasted pine kernels

Fresh herbs for garnish

1 garlic clove

Method

This dish can be prepared the day before, so all the ingredients are nicely marinated and chilled, leaving only the goat's cheese to cook and the dish to assemble.

To make the tomato compote, place a pan of water on the heat and bring to the boil. Make a small cut on the top of each tomato and plunge them in the boiling water for about 10 seconds. Remove and drop them into a bowl of cold water to cool. Once cooled, take off the skins, de-seed and reserve for later.

Pour the olive oil into a saucepan and cook the chopped onions on a low heat until they become soft. Add the white wine vinegar, fresh tomato, tomato purée, ground cumin, 4 tablespoons of water and put the lid on the top of the saucepan. Cook the compote very slowly until the tomatoes become mushy and a jam-like consistency is achieved. Season and allow to cool.

Place the peppers on a roasting tray, season and roast them in a preheated oven 190C/375F/ Gas 5 turning once, until the skin becomes slightly brown. Allow them to cool, remove the skins, de-seed and cut into large strips.

To make the basil pesto, put olive oil, basil, garlic and roasted pine kernels into a food processor and blend until all the ingredients are mixed well, then check seasoning. Place all the ingredients in the fridge until needed.

To prepared the goat's cheese, place some honey and sesame seeds on two different plates. Dip the sliced goat's cheese into the honey and then into the sesame seeds and place on a tray until needed.

Preheat the oven to 190C/375F/Gas 5. Cut the French sticks into thin slices, brush with a little olive oil and place in the oven until slightly crisp. Place the coated goat's cheese on top of the bread and return to the oven until the cheese becomes soft and the sesame seeds are golden brown.

To serve, spoon some of the tomato compote in the middle of the plate, add some strips of chilled peppers, place the goat's cheese in the middle of the plate, drizzle the plate with the fresh pesto and drop a few fresh herb leaves around the plate.

Serve straight away.

What a lovely colourful plate – full of flavour – you should be proud of yourself.

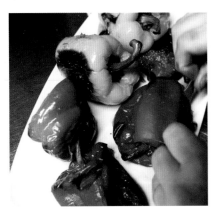   

Poire Farcie A Ma Façon
Pear risotto my way

What a great starter this is. The tanginess of the goat's cheese, the smooth taste of the mushrooms and the sweetness of the cranberry and poached pear give you outstanding flavours that complement each other so well.

To make the dish easier to assemble, I precook all the ingredients separately and bring them together at the last moment.

Ingredients

4 large pears

2 shallots (finely chopped)

175g risotto rice

25 mushrooms (300g)

1 clove garlic

2 tsp cranberry jelly

4 slices goat's cheese
(100g each crumbled)

Salt and pepper

½ to ¾ ltr vegetable stock
(1 vegetable stock cube)

4 tbsp granulated sugar

250ml balsamic vinegar

300ml red wine

Method

To prepare the pears, peel them (try to keep the stalks on), place in a deep saucepan, cover them completely with the red wine, sugar, balsamic vinegar and water if necessary. Cook slowly on a low heat for 10 to 15 minutes until the pears feel soft when tested with a knife.

Remove the pear and reduce the cooking juices until the sauce becomes syrupy. Allow to cool and reserve until needed.

Heat a little oil in a large frying pan, add the chopped shallots and cook them slowly for about 5 minutes until they become soft but not coloured. Add the risotto rice, cook for another 1 or 2 minutes without catching the bottom of your pan. Add a ladle of the hot vegetable stock and allow the rice to absorb most of the stock before adding another one. Continue this procedure for around 8 minutes (the risotto should remain quiet hard), then transfer the slightly undercooked risotto onto a flat tray to stop the cooking process, and place it somewhere cold (such as a window sill) until needed.

Melt the butter in a large frying pan over a medium heat. Once melted, add the chopped mushrooms and increase the heat to high. When the mushrooms are tender, add the chopped garlic and transfer them into a bowl until needed.

Take the cold pears, cut off the bottom, to make them easy to stand up, and remove the core. Place them in a small dish and microwave to warm them slightly at the last moment when the risotto is ready.

In a large thick bottomed saucepan add a ladle of hot vegetable stock and any juice from cooking the mushrooms, add the risotto and gently warm through. Add the mushrooms and if needed, continue adding a few more ladles of stock until the risotto is cooked. Check for seasoning, remove from the heat and add the crumbled goat's cheese and the cranberry jelly to your mix.

To serve, put a couple of spoons of risotto in the middle of the plate, place the warm poached pear on the top of your risotto and drizzle some pear/balsamic syrup around the plate.

That is a pretty plate – isn't it!

Poisson Poëlé A La Fricassée De Légumes Verts
Pan fried sea bass with green vegetables

This is a great starter which also can be served as a main course. You can use any fish you want; the most important thing for this dish is to make sure you do not overcook the fish or the green vegetables as you want the peas and asparagus to remain bright green. This is a simple dish where the ingredients have to be the best to achieve the best results, and where timing is of the essence to a successful dish!

Ingredients

4oz fillet fish
(sea-bass, salmon, etc)

200g peas

8 asparagus spears

12 sun-dried tomatoes
(optional)

8 large oyster mushrooms
(or any kind of mushrooms)

Garlic and vanilla sauce
_____

1 garlic bulb

½ vanilla pod

1 shallot (finely chopped)

Juice ½ lemon

½ glass white wine

250ml whipping cream

Salt and pepper

Olive oil

Knob of butter

Method

To make the sauce, place the whole garlic bulb in a preheated oven 170C/325F/Gas 3 for about 10 minutes (the garlic bulb should be soft to touch when cooked).

Add the finely chopped shallot, lemon juice and white wine to a saucepan and reduce the liquid by ⅔ then add ¾ of the cream. Add the whole roasted garlic bulb and the vanilla pod and reduce again until the sauce becomes syrupy. Blend the sauce with a hand blender, pass it through a fine sieve and reserve until needed.

Peel the asparagus and boil them in salted water for 1 minute (depending on the size) then plunge into very cold water to help keep them nice and green.

Prepare two hot frying pans. One for the fish and one for the vegetables.

Add a few drops of olive oil to a hot frying pan, season the sea-bass and cook it skin down for 1 minute, until the skin is crispy, then turn the fish over and cook for another minute depending on the thickness.

In another frying pan add a knob of butter and a drop of oil and fry the mushrooms, then add the asparagus and peas and a pinch of salt and pepper.

Slowly bring the sauce back to temperature.

To serve, place 2 or 3 spoons of the vegetables on a plate, place your fillet of fish on the top and add a drizzle of sauce around the plate.

A few leaves of parsley, dill, chopped chives or sundried tomato can be added to give you a lovely contrast of colour.

Great dish to set the tone of your cooking ability.

Les Plats | Main Course

Visual delights that dance on your taste buds and leave you smiling, happy and content.

Magret De Canard Au Balsamic, Orange Et Poivres Verts

Duck with orange and green peppercorns and a balsamic reduction

It took me about six years to put duck breast on my menu. I couldn't find the right duck breast, most of them used to come from France and they were frozen, a recipe for disaster, and most people wanted to eat them well done. Nowadays, a good English duck is freely available. Gressingham is always a good quality bird. To get a great result from a duck breast, cook to medium and most importantly, let it rest for 5 minutes to allow the meat to relax and keep it nice and pink!

Ingredients

4 x 8 oz medium duck breasts

Dauphinoise potatoes

2kg potatoes (peeled)

200ml milk

800ml whipping cream

Salt and pepper

2 garlic cloves
(peeled and crushed)

Braised red cabbage

1 red cabbage (around 800g)

50ml vegetable oil

100ml red or white wine
vinegar

2 apples (peeled and cubed)

200g dry fruits
(sultanas, apricots etc.)

4tsp granulated sugar

200ml water

Sauce

200ml balsamic vinegar

2 oranges

1 handful green peppercorns

500ml beef or chicken stock*

Method

To make the dauphinoise potatoes, bring the cream, milk, crushed garlic, salt and pepper to the boil. Cut the potato very thinly (use a mandoline slicer if you have one) and add to the hot garlic cream. Mix well and pour the potato mixture into a roasting dish or gratin dish.

Cover in greaseproof paper, place in a preheated oven 160C/325F/Gas 3 and cook for about 30/40 minutes. Check every 10 minutes and remove from the oven when cooked. Carefully place a flat tray over the cooked potato and add a weight on top so that the dauphinoise is pressed down. Allow to cool and leave in the fridge until the following day.

To make the braised red cabbage, pour the water into a large saucepan, add the sugar and reduce by ⅔ until the water becomes slight syrupy. Add the chopped red cabbage, place a lid on top and cook over a low heat for 20 minutes. When nearly cooked, add the vinegar, dry fruits, fresh fruit and olive oil and cook for a further 10 minutes until the cabbage is soft. Check the seasoning and reserve until needed.

To make the sauce, in a saucepan pour the balsamic vinegar and the zest of two oranges and reduce. Add the juice of the 2 oranges, the stock, and reduce until it becomes syrupy (the sauce should coat the back of a spoon when ready).

Add the green peppercorns and the sauce is ready.

Remove the dauphinoise potato from the fridge and using a pastry cutter, cut into individual portions. Place them on a baking tray and cook in a preheated oven 180C/350F/Gas 4 for about 8 minutes.

Gently warm the braised cabbage in a saucepan or microwave.

To cook the duck breasts, in a hot pan or roasting tray that can go in the oven, place the breasts skin down (this will make the skin nice and crispy). Transfer to the oven 200C/400F/Gas 6, for about 8 minutes. When ready, leave for 5 minutes to rest. Slice the duck just before serving, as it will release some blood after slicing.

To serve, place the red cabbage and the round dauphinoise potato on the plate. Pour the sauce next to the cabbage and place the finely sliced hot duck breast on the cabbage to finish.

You did a great job!

*I use Essential Cuisine stock, available to purchase online at **www.essentialcuisine.com/homechef** or at reputable farm shops and delis, see page 88

Serves 4

Filet De Boeuf Farci Au Bleu

Fillet of beef filled with blue cheese

When writing this book, I didn't think of including a beef dish, as I didn't want to put a recipe involving a braising beef dish or a steak with a sauce on the top, but this beef dish is very popular at the restaurant.

Ingredients

4 x 6oz fillet of beef (taken from the middle of the fillet)

8 nice thin slices pancetta

200g cream cheese

200g blue cheese

1 tsp cracked pepper

200g shallot (finely chopped)

100g butter

100ml vegetable oil

100ml port

2 tbsp beef stock*

Tarragon or thyme

4 large jacket or Maris Piper potatoes (250g peeled)

Baby carrots

100g wild mushroom or oyster mushrooms

2 x 200g bags spinach

3 tbsp vegetable oil and 3 tbsp of plain flour mixed together to form a paste

A great dish full of powerful flavours.

Method

To make the rosti potato, line a thin roasting tray with greaseproof paper (try to use good quality greaseproof paper as the cheaper versions will stick) then coat the lining with 2 tablespoons of vegetable oil. Grate the potatoes using the largest hole of a grater and spread them over the oiled paper to approximately 1cm thick by 10cm square.

Roast in the oven at 200C/400F/Gas 6 for about 10 to 14 minutes, until the potato becomes golden brown and slightly soft. Allow to cool down for 15 minutes then roll the potato, removing the greaseproof paper. Roll up the potato in clingfilm and tightly knot each end to resemble a Christmas cracker. Leave in the fridge until needed.

To make the filling, mix the cream cheese and blue cheese together.

To prepare the meat, with the help of a sharp knife, cut a flap in the top of each fillet, being careful not to cut through to the bottom and leaving the flap attached. Fill each pocket with the cheese filling and replace the flap to keep the filling inside. Sprinkle them with cracked pepper, wrap the pancetta around each fillet and reserve until needed.

Cook the carrots in some salted boiling water for about 3 minutes depending on their size. Refresh them in cold water, dry and reserve them for later. Repeat the process with the spinach (wash well beforehand if necessary) and boil for about 10 seconds only, dry well on kitchen paper and reserve.

Prepare the mushrooms cutting them in two if necessary. In a large frying pan heat 30g of butter and 1 tablespoon of oil over a medium heat.

When hot, add the mushrooms and toss them around for 5 minutes on a high heat until they become shiny and soft. Reserve until needed.

To make the sauce, in a thick bottomed saucepan and over a medium heat, add 20g of butter and 2 tablespoons of oil. When hot, add the chopped shallots and cook them for about 20 minutes until they become very soft and quite dark (without burning them). Add the port and reduce by ½. Add 200ml of water and 2 tablespoons of the stock, reduce by ⅓ and leave to cool. If the sauce is too runny bring it back to the boil and add a few drops of paste made from the flour and oil. Repeat the operation until you get the sauce to the right consistency.

To complete the dish is all about timing. First, bring the sauce back to the heat and add some chopped tarragon or thyme. If required, add some vegetable oil and flour paste to obtain the correct consistency.

In a large hot frying pan or medium roasting tray, add 50g of butter and 1 tablespoon of oil. Place the fillet in the pan and place in a preheated oven 240C/475F/ Gas 9 or under a hot grill for about 5 minutes. Take the potato roulade out of the fridge and cut into 4 x 2cm thick slices. Place them onto a thin, oil coated oven tray and cook in the oven for about 3 minutes, turning them after 2 minutes. When you see the blue cheese starting to ooze out of the fillets, remove from the oven and allow to rest for 3 minutes.

Heat 40g of butter in a saucepan and when hot, add the carrots, mushrooms and the spinach and toss for 4 minutes to warm through. Check the seasoning and the dish is ready to be served. To serve, remove any excess water from the spinach and place the vegetables in the middle of the plate. Place the potato rosti on top of spinach, add the steak, the vegetables and finish with the sauce.

*I use Essential Cuisine stock, available to purchase online at www.essentialcuisine.com/homechef or at reputable farm shops and delis, see page 88

Saumon Poëlé Fondue De Tomates Et Basilic
Salmon with tomato and basil compote and crushed potatoes

This is a dish I was served in a lovely Cheshire gastro pub during a wine tasting and I've got to say, I love it. I've made a few amendments, but I love the taste and the plate is so colourful. I serve it with crushed potatoes and tomato compote, but you can add more vegetables such as grilled asparagus or courgette if you prefer.

Make sure the crushed potatoes, tomato compote and the basil are hot and ready to be served before you start cooking the salmon so you can concentrate on cooking the salmon to perfection!

Ingredients

4 x 200g salmon fillets

100g flour

100ml extra virgin oil

10 ripe fresh tomatoes (chopped)

1 small tin tomatoes (chopped)

10 black olives

1 dessert spoon of granulated sugar

2 small chorizos

1 white onion

Crushed potatoes

30 medium new potatoes

2 large white onions

6 garlic cloves (peeled)

100ml extra olive oil

1 small bunch parsley (chopped)

Juice of ½ lemon

Basil sauce

100ml white wine

2 dessert spoons white wine vinegar

1 good handful fresh basil

100ml whipping cream

1 shallot (chopped)

Method

To make the tomato compote, cut a cross on the top of each tomato and drop them in boiling water for 10 seconds. Remove them and place them in very iced cold water to cool them down quickly. Peel them, cut them in half and remove the seeds.

Pour the olive oil into a saucepan and add the chopped onions and de-seeded tomatoes and cook for 5 minutes on a low heat. Add the chopped tinned tomatoes, sugar, cubed chorizo and black olives and cook for 20 minutes until the mix resembles tomato jam. Reserve until needed.

To make the basil sauce, place the chopped shallot, white wine and vinegar in a saucepan and reduce by ⅔. Add the cream and slowly reduce again until the correct consistency is achieved. Add the fresh basil and, using a hand blender, blend and then pass through a fine sieve. Reserve until needed.

To make the crushed potatoes, finely chop the onions, place them in a medium saucepan, add the olive oil and crushed cloves of garlic and cook over a low heat for about 20 minutes until very tender.

When cooked, transfer to a mixing bowl and reserve until needed.

Boil the new potatoes in salt water until slightly over cooked. Refresh them in cold water, dry off and peel. Add them to the onion mix with the chopped parsley, lemon juice and salt and pepper.

Using your hands, roughly crush the potatoes and mix everything together. Reserve in the fridge until needed.

To serve, gently warm the tomato compote through.

Cover the bowl of crushed potato with cling film and reheat in the microwave.

Place the flour on a tray or plate and season. Place the salmon fillets on the flour, skin side down.

In a large frying pan or ovenproof pan, heat a dash of olive oil. When the pan is hot, season and cook the fillets, skin down, for about 1 minute. Gently turn over and cook on medium heat for another 5 minutes – depending on the thickness of the fish. The fish will be cooked when the flesh becomes firm to touch. You can test if the fish is cooked by making a small incision in the fillet to check inside.

Reheat the basil sauce on a low heat and add a little water if it appears too thick. Do not let it boil, otherwise the sauce could split.

Place a stainless steel ring in the middle of a plate and fill it with the crushed potato to keep the shape. Remove the ring and add some tomato compote on top of the potato. Place the salmon on top and pour some of the basil sauce around the plate.

What a great colourful dish!

Gigonette D'Agneau Provençal

Lamb shank with roasted vegetables and mash

The first time I ate lamb shank was in the late 80s in a hotel in Carlisle. It was served glazed in honey and mint and I loved it straight away. It took me a few years to include them on my menu but when I did it was an immediate success at the restaurant. Years have passed and I still serve them exactly the same way as 25 years ago; why change anything?

I like to serve the lamb in a garlic, rosemary and tomato sauce. I love rosemary; it reminds me of the South of France where my house was full of it and the smell was so strong. I serve the gigonette with roasted Mediterranean vegetables and mashed potato and sometimes I add wholegrain mustard or spring onion to the mash to change the taste slightly.

Ingredients

4 lamb shank (1lb each)

Salt and pepper

Bunch of fresh rosemary

I whole garlic

140g or 5 tbsp tomato purée

A little oil

Roasted vegetables

1 red/yellow/green pepper

3 courgettes

2 red onions

1 handful black olives (optional)

20 cherry tomatoes

1 handful fresh basil

1 small aubergine

2 garlic bulbs (crushed)

70ml olive oil

3 tbsp olive oil

Salt and pepper
for the mash

2kg Maris Piper potatoes

100ml olive oil

Method

Bring 3 litres of water to the boil and add a handful of sea salt. Plunge the lamb shanks for 3 minutes (plunge only 2 at the time) this will help to keep the meat tight and on the bone.

Add a little oil to a roasting tray and place in a preheated the oven 240C/475F/Gas 9. Place the lamb in the tray, add the garlic, salt and pepper and roast them until they become nice and brown. After 20 minutes add the tomato purée and roast for another 5 minutes. Pour the water from the plunged lamb shanks into the roasting tray, add the fresh rosemary and reduce the heat to 200C/400F/Gas 6. Continue cooking for about 1 hour 45 minutes until the meat almost falls off the bone. Make sure the lamb shank sauce does not boil.

Leave the meat in the tray and let it rest for 20 minutes. Carefully remove them from the cooking juice and place them on a flat tray to cool down.

Pass the sauce through a fine sieve and reduce it until you are happy with the taste. Reserve for later.

To cook the roasted vegetables, de-seed the peppers, peel the onions and cut all the vegetables into quarters. Place the cut vegetables (except the courgette) onto a roasting tray, add the garlic, fresh herbs, salt, pepper and olive oil and mix well. Place in a hot oven 200C/400F/Gas 6 and cook for about 15 minutes, stirring every 5 minutes.

During the last 5 minutes, add the courgettes, cherry tomatoes and black olives, and reserve for later.

To make the mashed potato, peel and boil the potato in salted water for about 30 minutes until very soft. Remove from the water and allow them to dry before mashing. Check the seasoning, add 50ml of olive oil and reserve until later.

Bring the sauce back to the boil. Reduce the heat and gently place the lamb shanks into the sauce to heat them through. This should take about 25 minutes.

Reheat the vegetables in the oven for about 10 minutes at 170C/325F/Gas 3.

Reheat the mash in the microwave, add the remaining 50ml of olive oil and mix until light and fluffy using a hand mixer.

To serve, place the roasted vegetables on the outside of the plate, spoon on the mashed potato in the middle, place the lamb shank on the top and pour over the sauce.

A classic!

Filet De Sole Aux Sésames
Sole fillets with sesame

This a quick dish, full of north African flavours. Here I've used lots of different beans to make a colourful plate but you can use any favourite bean. I've also used tins of beans but nothing is better than fresh beans.

There are no potatoes in this recipe because I don't think it needs any.

I generally use lemon sole or plaice but you can use monkfish (if you use monkfish, make sure you cut them into thin medallions to make the cooking process easier).

To flavour this dish I use harissa paste, which is easily available in supermarkets. It is a paste made mainly from tomato and chilli and it is quite hot but very tasty if used properly.

Ingredients

4 lemon sole fillets (or 6oz each plaice fillet)

2 tsp sesame seeds

3 tbsp plain flour

150g butter

50ml olive oil

Salt and pepper

1½ tsp harissa paste
(add more if you like it hotter)

1 tin butter beans 200g

1 tin runner beans 200g

1 tin kidney beans 200g

1 tin flageolet beans 200g

1 small bunch coriander

1 pkt rocket salad leaves

Method

Melt 100g of butter and add ¼ teaspoon of harissa paste. Taste it and add more if you like it hotter, then reserve until needed.

Open the tins of beans, wash them under cold water for about 3 minutes and place them into a sieve to remove the water.

Mix the flour, sesame seeds and salt and pepper together and place it on a large plate.

Cut the lemon sole into large goujons and reserve until needed.

To complete the dish you need two large non stick pans; one for the fish and one for the beans.

Place the lemon sole goujons in the flour and sesame seeds, mix and gently coat them. Melt 40g of butter and 2 dessert spoons of olive oil in the pan over a medium heat and place the lemon goujons in the pan. Cook them for about 1 minute, depending on the size, and gently turn them over until they become golden in colour. This should not take more than five minutes.

Remove and place them onto kitchen paper to absorb the excess oil. Add the remaining cooking liquor to the beans.

Heat the harissa butter and 2 spoons of olive oil in the other pan and, when the butter begins to bubble, add all the beans with the cooking liquor from the fish (as above), mix together and heat well.

Just before serving the bean mix, add the juice of the lemon (or lime), add chopped coriander and rocket salad, add more olive oil or a drop of water if the bean mix looks a bit dry. Place the goujon of lemon sole on top of the beans and there you have it!

What can be easier than this dish? I know – phone 01925 753657 and ask for a table for 4!

Serves 4

Duo De Coquelet A L'Estragon
Baby chicken with roasted vegetables

This is such a great dish. We don't use baby chickens enough; they are so moist and sweet. I first made this dish at home to make sure the recipe worked, and I have to say, my guests loved it. Poussin, or baby chicken, is wildly available in supermarkets but it can be a bit difficult to remove the legs and breast from the bird. I would always advise that you ask your butcher to do it for you, but always ask him to give you the carcass to make the sauce. We will serve the dish with a beautiful sweet chicken jus.

Ingredients

4 baby chickens

8 slices Parma ham

A large handful of chopped fresh tarragon (around 150g. Keep 50g to mix with the vegetables)

500ml cooking oil

Salt and pepper

For the stock

1 small carrot

1 celery stick

I red onion

1tbsp tomato purée

1 glass white wine

4 dessert spoons plain flour and vegetable oil mixed to a paste

Vegetables

1 butternut squash (around 800g weight)

8 asparagus

20 mangetout

8 baby sweetcorn

50g butter

12 boiled new potatoes (cut in half)

A great plate of food!

Method

The dish has 3 stages: first, get the poussin leg cooked and the breast wrapped in Parma ham; second, get the vegetables prepared and cooked; third, make the tarragon sauce. To make the sauce, preheat the oven to 200C/400F/Gas 6. Add a dessert spoon of vegetable oil to a medium sized roasting tray, place the poussin carcasses, chopped carrot, celery and chopped red onion, and roast for about 15 minutes. Stir every 5 minutes until the bones and vegetables are slightly brown, add the tomato purée and roast for another 5 minutes.

Transfer everything to a large saucepan. Pour the glass of wine into the roasting tin, stir well then transfer the liquid to the poussin bone and vegetables. Add enough water to cover the vegetables and simmer the stock for about 20 minutes, pressing the bones with the back of a spoon to get the flavour out. When reduced, pass through a fine sieve. Bring the liquid back to the boil, add some oil and flour to thicken the sauce slightly and reserve for later.

To prepare the vegetables, keep the mangetout raw but plunge the asparagus in boiling salted water for 1 minute, then plunge them straight into cold water. Repeat the process with the sweet corn. Peel the butternut squash, remove the inside, and cut it into 1 cm thick cubes and keep it raw until needed. To prepare the poussin, place the legs in a thick bottomed saucepan and cover with vegetable oil, cook them very slowly for about 20 minutes - do not bring the oil to the boil. (The kitchen term for this is making chicken leg confit.) To check if they are cooked, you should be able to pass a knife through without too much resistance. When ready, take them out of the oil and reserve for later. Place a slice of Parma ham on a clean work top and wrap it around the boneless baby chicken breast. Repeat until all the breasts are done and reserve until needed.

Over a medium flame, pour 3 dessert spoons of oil into a large thin roasting tray, add the new potatoes and place the leg confit on top of the potatoes. Place the wrapped poussin directly onto the bottom of the roasting tray (so they will become nice and crispy when cooked) and roast in a preheated oven 240C/475F/ Gas 9 for 6 minutes. When cooked, I like to put the legs in the sauce to ensure they're hot enough. Meanwhile, put 50g of butter in a frying pan over a medium heat. When hot, add the butternut squash and a bit of seasoning and cook them for about 1 minute each side until golden in colour. Turn the heat to low and continue to cook for a couple of minutes until they become soft. Reserve for later and keep warm by covering with a piece of foil.

Reheat the sauce, and at the last moment add the fresh chopped tarragon. Plunge all the vegetables into boiling water for 1 minute. Drain them and toss them in a knob of butter. Season and add the chopped tarragon.

To serve, place the blanched vegetables, pan fried butternut squash, and new potatoes on a plate. Arrange the breast on top of the vegetables, remove the leg from the sauce and arrange next to the breast, then drizzle the sauce all around the plate.

Poulet A La Bourguignone
Stuffed pan-fried chicken breast

This is a dish I served on Mother's Day and I really liked the look of it. It is a dish with a full smoky flavour - from the pancetta - and the velvety creamy tarragon sauce complements it well. Chicken is always a good dish to serve. You can also use guinea fowl or corn fed chicken breast.

This dish consists of pan fried chicken breast, filled with flavoured cream cheese and served on a bed of caramelised baby onions with green beans, mushrooms, pancetta and carrots, accompanied with a creamy tarragon sauce.

Ingredients

4 chicken breasts

½ kg carrots (peeled)

1 tbsp white sugar

1 pinch cracked pepper

12 baby onions (peeled)

1 lb pancetta (cubed)

12 Chestnut or Paris mushrooms (cut in half)

200g French beans (cut in half)

1 glass white wine

½ cube chicken stock or 1 tbsp of chicken stock powder*

250ml whipping cream

200g cream cheese

3 spring onions (chopped)

10 chopped sun-dried tomatoes (optional)

12 medium boiled new potatoes (cut in half)

1 large bunch fresh tarragon (chopped)

Butter and olive oil

½ tsp granulated sugar

Method

Peel the carrots, dice them into cubes and place them in a saucepan. Half cover with boiling water, add the sugar and cracked pepper, and cook them until tender. Drain and set aside in a bowl for later.

In a saucepan, bring some salted water to the boil and cook the French beans for 1 minute. Remove and plunge them straight away into cold water to help maintain the colour. Repeat the process with the baby onions, but cook them for 3 minutes.

After cooking, place the vegetables on kitchen paper and dry thoroughly.

In a large frying pan, add the butter and sugar and a dash of olive oil. When hot, add the onions and cook on a medium heat, stirring well until they become caramelised. Set aside until needed later.

Fry the cubed pancetta in a few drops of oil until it browns, and reserve for later. In the same pan, fry the mushrooms and reserve for later.

To prepare the chicken, mix together the finely chopped spring onion, sun-dried tomato and cream cheese in a mixing bowl. With the help of a sharp knife, cut a pocket in each chicken breast, spoon the cheese filling inside and close to prevent the filling from escaping during cooking.

To make the tarragon sauce, pour a glass of white wine into a saucepan and reduce by ⅔. Add a glass of water and the chicken stock cube and reduce again by ⅔. Add the cream and reduce until the sauce starts to thicken. Remove from the heat and set aside until needed.

In a large hot ovenproof pan, pour a little oil and add a knob of butter. Place the chicken breasts (cream cheese pocket side up) and cook for about 8 minutes 200C/400F/Gas 6, depending on the weight of each breast.

In a large wok or large non-stick frying pan, add a knob of butter and olive oil, place the new potatoes (cut in ½) and fry them in the hot pan, stirring well until they start to colour. Add the carrot, onion, pancetta, mushrooms and French beans, stir well to heat through (allow 5 minutes for cooking process).

Bring the sauce back to the heat, add the tarragon and season.

To serve, place a generous portion of the mixed vegetables in the middle of the plate, place the chicken breast on the top and finish with the creamy tarragon sauce.

A dish to please the ladies!

*I use Essential Cuisine stock, available to purchase online at www.essentialcuisine.com/homechef or at reputable farm shops and delis, see page 88

Cabillaud Au Risotto Du Jardin
Cod with green vegetable risotto

This is a dish which is always well received. The creamy risotto complements the meaty flesh of the cod. I serve this dish with a drizzle of extra olive oil and lemon juice - very simple, but perfect. You can also serve this risotto on its own as a starter. Try to not serve too much risotto for this dish in order to keep it nice, light and tidy on the plate.

I always cook my risotto in two stages - it makes the timing of the dish much easier. To cook a risotto from start to finish should take about 15 minutes, but sometimes it takes longer, so half cooking the risotto should make it easier for you.

Ingredients

4 x 7oz cod fillets

50g plain flour
(for dusting the fish)

60g butter

150g leek
(washed well and chopped)

175g Arborio rice

200g grated Parmesan

200g onions (diced)

200g peas

12 small asparagus

100ml extra olive oil

600ml vegetable stock
(1 vegetable cube per
ltr of water)

1 lemon

1 small bunch chives (chopped)

Method

Have the litre of vegetable stock hot when you start to make the risotto.

Over a medium heat, melt the butter in a saucepan and add the chopped onion and cook for about 5 minutes until the onion is nice and soft. Add the risotto rice and cook for another minute.

Pour in a ladle of stock and allow the rice to absorb most of the stock before adding another ladleful. Continue this process for 10 minutes then remove the pan away from the heat. You should have used 400-500ml of the vegetable stock and the risotto should still be hard. Turn the risotto out onto a large flat tray and allow to cool.

Blanch the asparagus in boiling water for 2 minutes, refresh them in cold ice water and reserve until needed.

Reheat the vegetable stock.

In a large thick-bottomed saucepan, melt 50g of butter and slowly cook the leeks until they become very soft. Add a ladle of vegetable stock, then the cold risotto and mix well.

Begin to cook the fish.

Place some extra olive oil in a large frying pan, dust the cod with flour and cook skin side down on a medium heat for about 3 minutes. Carefully turn the fish over and cook for another 3 minutes depending on the thickness of the fish. Turn the heat off and leave the fish in the pan until needed.

Continue to cook the risotto as before, allowing the rice to absorb the stock before adding another ladle. When the risotto is nearly ready, gradually add some grated Parmesan then add the asparagus, peas and more Parmesan. Check for seasoning and remove from the heat.

To serve, spoon the risotto into the middle of the plate and place the cod fillet on top of the risotto. Squeeze the juice of the lemon in the pan where you cooked the cod and drizzle the cooking liquor on top of the fish. Top the fish with the finely chopped chives.

What a great dish mon jardin sur l'assiette!

Serves 4

Ragoût De Chevreuil A La Poire
Braised venison shoulder in a balsamic and pear sauce

This is a great winter dish. I like to serve it with a creamy, buttery, full of calories, mashed potato. Most of the venison comes from Scotland and it is a lovely flavoured red meat. I suggest you order it a couple of days in advance from your butcher. You should ask him for 1.5 kg of young venison shoulder cut into 200g chunks. Try fillet of venison for a treat, it's absolutely beautiful.

Ingredients

1.5 kg venison shoulder

5 shallots 400g (chopped)

2 carrots (chopped)

1 celery head (chopped)

2 cloves of garlic

300ml balsamic vinegar

300ml red wine

100g tomato purée

1 x 400g tin pears

½ ltr cranberry juice

3 tbsp vegetable oil and 3 tbsp of plain flour mixed together

For the mash

2kg potatoes (Maris Pipers are good)

100g butter

1 bunch spring onion (finely chopped)

Salt and pepper

Method

Heat a large pan until it is very hot then add a film of oil. Season the chunks of venison, fry them for about 3 minutes to seal and reserve. When all the venison has been sealed, remove the excess oil from the pan and reduce the heat to medium. Add the shallots and stir them until they colour and become soft, then add the carrots, garlic, celery and tomato purée.

Add the balsamic vinegar and reduce by ⅔, then add the red wine and reduce again by ⅔. Place the chunks of venison back in a pan. Pour in the juice of the pears and add some cranberry juice until all the meat is submerged. Bring back up to heat, put a lid on the pan and reduce the heat to as low as possible and cook for about 1½ hours.

Check it every 20 minutes, and if necessary, top up with cranberry juice or water to keep the venison submerged. Do not allow the liquid to boil as this will overcook the meat and make it tough (a good casserole takes time). To check if the venison is cooked, gently press the meat with your finger – it should be soft and start to fall apart. At this stage, take the meat out of the sauce and place on a tray. Pass the sauce through a sieve and return it back to a medium heat to reduce until a velvety, sweet taste is achieved.

If the sauce is still a bit runny, bring it back to the boil and add the vegetable oil and flour paste a little at a time until it becomes thicker. Add the chopped pear to the sauce and check for seasoning.

While the venison is cooking, peel the potatoes, cut them equally in half and bring them slowly to the boil in 2 litres of salted water and cook them for about 30 to 40 minutes.

Transfer them to a colander and allow them to dry for a few minutes. Mash them and add 50g of melted butter. Check the seasoning and transfer the mash to a microwavable bowl.

Bring the sauce back to the boil, add the braised venison and reduce the heat to allow the meat to heat through. Warm the mash in a microwave, transfer it to a thick bottomed saucepan, add the chopped spring onion and another 50g of melted butter and whisk it with a hand whisk to make it lighter.

To serve, spoon a portion of the mash into the middle of the plate, add a large helping of the venison and top with the sauce.

Vive l'Ecosse!

Bar Au Gateau De Crabe Et Crevettes Grises
Sea bass with thai shrimp and crab cakes

This a great Thai dish full of clean and fresh flavours, which is why I love it. The only downside is the vast quantities of ingredients you require. I serve the dish with fresh samphire, which is a seaweed, also called the asparagus of the sea. It is a bit salty but goes great with fish. The ingredients below are only a guide. You may prefer it more or less spicy, in which case, you would adapt the amount of chilli to your taste. You can also serve the crab and shrimp cake as a starter.

Ingredients

6 sea bass fillets (from a fish 500g to 600g)

200g fresh samphire

20ml sesame oil

Thai crab cakes

200g shrimps

300g crab meat

3 spring onions (finely chopped)

½ bunch fresh coriander (chopped)

1 lemon (juice and zest)

30g fresh ginger (chopped)

20g to 30g fresh red chillies (chopped) biggest you can find

3 tbsp ketchup

Salt and pepper

1 medium jacket potato (cooked to make 200g dry mash)

200g white breadcrumbs (or Japanese breadcrumbs)

Method

To make the Thai crab cakes

Place all the ingredients in a large mixing bowl and fold gently. If the mix feels a bit too moist, add more breadcrumbs and taste for seasoning. When the mixture is to your satisfaction, mould it into 6 round cakes and place in the fridge until needed.

Thai sauce

4 sticks chopped lemon grass (crushed in a mortar and pestle)
50g shallots (finely chopped)
50g red chillies (finely chopped)
80g ginger (finely chopped)
1 measure sweet sherry
100ml water
2 tbsp light soy sauce
3 tbsp sesame oil
1 dash Thai fish sauce (optional)
2 tins coconut milk
½ chicken cube or ¾ tbsp chicken stock powder*
½ cup water
bunch fresh coriander (chopped)
1 bunch spring onion (chopped)
1 tbsp granulated sugar (optional)
3 tbsp vegetable oil and 3 tbsp plain flour mixed together to a paste

To make the sauce

Gently heat the sesame oil in a large saucepan, add the chopped shallots, ginger, chillies and lemon grass. Cook slowly for a few minutes then add the sweet sherry and reduce by half. Add the ½ cup of water and chicken stock and reduce by half again.

Pour in the coconut milk, soy sauce and fish sauce and reduce again for a few more minutes.

When you are happy with the taste, add a little of the oil and flour paste to thicken the sauce. The sauce may need a little more chilli, ginger, lemon grass or sugar, just add to suit your taste.

When ready, remove all the woody lemon grass but do not pass through a sieve. The coriander and spring onion will be added just before serving.

Plunge the samphire into boiling water for about 5 seconds then straight away into iced cold water. Dry and reserve until needed. To complete the dish, bring the sauce slowly back to the heat ready to be served.

Add 20ml of sesame oil to a hot wok and quickly reheat the samphire for 2 minutes. Lightly flour the Thai crab cakes and fry until they are slightly coloured on both sides, then bake them in the oven for about 3 minutes in a preheated oven 180C/350F/Gas 4.

Lightly flour the skin of the seabass. Add a dash of olive oil to a pan and cook for 2 minutes on each side.

To serve, place the samphire in the middle of the plate, add the crab and shrimp cake, then the seabass. Add the chopped coriander and spring onion to the sauce and pour it around the plate.

Et voilà un petit goût de Thaïlande.

*I use Essential Cuisine stock, available to purchase online at www.essentialcuisine.com/homechef or at reputable farm shops and delis, see page 88

Roulade D'Agneau Façon Bohème

La Boheme lamb roulade

Ingredients

1 x 1.5kg lamb shoulder boned and tied

2 carrots (chopped)

2 white onions (chopped)

1 head of celery (chopped)

50ml olive oil

4 cloves garlic

4 sprigs rosemary (around 150g)

1 tbsp tomato purée (around 140g)

2.5 ltr water

1 tsp cumin

4 medium sliced red onions (600g)

3 tbsp ketchup

1 sprig rosemary (finely chopped around 100g)

250g dried apricots (chopped)

6 large potatoes (around 1.8kg when peeled)

Root vegetables

1 large swede

8 asparagus

2 large parsnips

2 large carrots

1 mooli

2 tbsp of granulated sugar

2 bunches curly parsley

75g butter

100ml olive oil

Phew, that was worth the effort! A great dish with multiple saveurs.

This dish is full of flavour and looks great on the plate. I advise you to cook the shoulder a day in advance and prepare all the vegetables a few hours before serving the dish.

Method

To cook the lamb, heat a little olive oil in a roasting tray over a medium heat. Season the lamb shoulder and cook it skin down for about 7 or 8 minutes until the skin becomes golden brown. Turn the lamb over and add the chopped white onions, celery and carrots and cook for about 5 more minutes.

With the lamb shoulder skin side up, add the tomato purée, rosemary and garlic and cover with about 2.5 litres of water. Place in a preheated oven 240C/475F/Gas 9 for about 30 minutes - until the water begins to boil - then reduce the temperature to 190C/375F/Gas 5 and continue to cook for another 1½ hours.

Turn the lamb over every 30 minutes and add more water if required. To prevent the lamb sauce from boiling during cooking, reduce the temperature of the oven. The lamb should be almost falling apart when cooked so allow it to cool down for 30 minutes before gently removing it from the stock. Place it on a flat tray and allow it to cool down further.

Pass the stock through a sieve, reduce until the sauce is syrupy and full of flavour, and reserve until needed.

While the lamb cooks, in a saucepan pour 3 tablespoons of olive oil, add the chopped red onion and cook gently until the onions become very soft. Add the ground cumin and cook for another 4 minutes. Set aside to cool down, then add the ketchup, rosemary and chopped apricots.

When the lamb is cool enough to handle, shred by hand, add to the red onion mixture and season. Place the mixture on some clingfilm and make into 2 or 3 sausage shapes (thickness of a rolling pin) and keep in the fridge until needed.

To make the potato roulade, take a large oven tray, cover with greaseproof paper and brush generously with oil. Peel the potatoes, slice them very thinly, (preferably with a mandolin slicer), cover the greaseproof paper with two layers of potatoes, season and place in the oven 200C/400F/Gas 6 for about 10 minutes, until the potato becomes soft and slightly brown.

Take out of the oven and let them cool for about 10 minutes. Once cooled, remove the cling film from the lamb sausage and place lengthways on top of the potatoes (still on greaseproof paper). Roll up tightly like a Swiss roll, cover in clingfilm and transfer to the fridge until needed.

To prepare the vegetables, peel and cut the vegetables to roughly the same shape and size (approximately little finger size) and keep them separate. In a large saucepan of boiling salted water, cook each vegetable individually (except the parsnips) to a slightly crunchy texture and plunge them in cold water. Dry them and reserve for later.

Pour 3 tablespoons of olive oil into a roasting tray and add the parsnips. Roast on the middle shelf in a preheated oven 200C/400F/Gas 6 until they become slightly brown in colour. Remove and reserve separately from the other vegetables for use later.

In a wok, heat up 3 tablespoons of olive oil and 50g of butter and add the vegetables (but not the parsnip). Add 2 tablespoons of sugar, mix well and cook until the vegetables become caramelised and shiny. Add the parsnip, chopped parsley and check for seasoning. Bring the heat right down. Slice the potato roulade into 2cm thick slices and place on a non-stick tray with a little oil in a preheated oven 200C/400F/Gas 6. Cook for about 3 minutes each side. Reheat the lamb sauce.

To serve, arrange a few spoons of the vegetables on a plate, add 2 slices of lamb and potato roulade and finish with the beautiful lamb sauce.

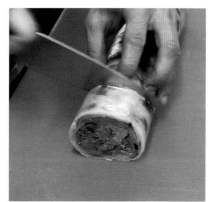

Les Desserts | Puds

Indulgent and delightful, you want to say no but always say yes. A good dessert is worth putting your diet on hold for.

Tarte Au Citron Coulis De Framboises

Lemon tart with raspberry coulis

This is one of my favourite sweets. I feel the very refreshing tangy lemon tart and coulis of raspberry is ideal for a typical hot summer's day in Manchester. You can also change the recipe slightly to 7 lemons and 1 lime to give you a great lemon and lime tart (zest the lime and add it to the mix).

Ingredients

Tarte au citron

8 lemons

250g white sugar

11 eggs

½ ltr cream

Raspberry coulis

3 punnets fresh raspberries

100g icing sugar

Method

To make the tart base, use frozen short-crust pastry or sweet pastry bought in.

Flour the inside of a 3.75cm deep tart ring with a removable base to allow the tart to release easily. Roll out the pastry to 5mm thick and place it carefully on the top of the tart base.

Gently ease the pastry into the tart ring and, without cutting off the excess, allow the pastry to rest in the fridge for at least an hour. This will ensure the case does not shrink later. Meanwhile, preheat the oven to 180C/350F/Gas 4.

Place greaseproof paper or foil onto the pastry case and fill with baking beans. Bake blind for about 15 minutes. Remove from the oven, remove the foil and baking beans and leave to settle for a few minutes.

Check for holes in the pastry case and if required fill them well with raw pastry. It is very important not to have any holes in the pastry or the lemon filling will seep out and ruin the dessert.

Bake for a further 5 minutes until nice and golden. Leave to cool down, and do not trim off the pastry overlap until the tart filling is added and cooked. To make the tart filling, zest 4

lemons and squeeze the juice of 8 lemons. Pass the lemon juice through a fine sieve, then place the lemon juice in a large bowl, add the eggs and sugar and whisk well.

Add the cream and gently pour the mixture into the blind-baked tart case. Place the tart in the oven 170C/325F/Gas 3 and bake for about 30 minutes until the tart does not wobble when shaken. If unsure, switch off the oven and leave the tart in for a further 15 minutes. When the tart is ready, allow it to cool down and then trim off the pastry overlap.

To make the raspberry coulis, this is best left to the last moment to maintain a fresh and slightly light coulis. Place 1 or 2 punnets of raspberries (depending on the punnet size) into a mixing bowl, add the icing sugar and whisk with a small hand blender. Depending on taste and consistency, you can add a bit of water if too thick, or more sugar if not sweet enough. Pass the coulis through a small sieve to remove the raspberry seeds.

To serve, cut the tart into 10 portions and pour a small amount of raspberry coulis alongside it. Add a few fresh raspberries and sprinkle with icing sugar.

All you now need is a sunny day in Manchester to complete the dish!

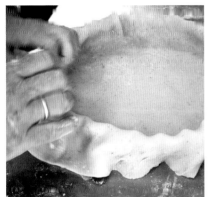

Crème Brûlée
Crème brûlée

What can I say about crème brûlée? It's difficult to please everyone, because people judge in different ways. I like mine slightly runny with a lot of beautiful vanilla seeds in a smooth mix, and I like to serve crème brûlée with shortbread or an almond tuile and a compote of fruit like strawberries or rhubarb.

The most important thing to a successful crème brûlée is the timing. Every oven is different, so try to keep a record of how long, and what temperature you cook at to monitor and master your baking.

Ingredients

700ml double cream

100ml milk

125g caster sugar

150g egg yolks

1 split vanilla pod

4 tbsp demerara sugar for brûlée topping

Method

In a large saucepan pour the cream, milk, half the caster sugar and vanilla pod (cut lengthways) and gently bring to the boil, reducing the heat once boiled. Gently whisk the egg yolks and the remaining sugar together, then add one ladleful of the boiling cream mixture and mix well. Mix in another ladleful of hot cream, slowly pour the egg mixture into the saucepan of boiling cream. Mix and then strain the mixture gently through a sieve to remove the vanilla pod. Pour the hot mix into the ramekins and fill to ¾ full.

Place in a deep roasting tray and fill with boiling water, to one-third of the height of the tray, and cook in the oven 140C/275F/Gas 1 for about 15 to 20 minutes.

To check if they are cooked, give them a little shake; the tops should wobble but remain a little firm. It's important to cook the crème brûlée on a slow heat, so if after 30 minutes they still don't look cooked, leave them in the oven but don't turn the oven heat up.

Too much heat will cook the egg yolk and the brûlée will split. When the crème brûlées are ready, leave to cool down.

For the topping

When ready to serve, sprinkle the chilled brûlée with brown sugar, and with the help of a gas burner (or grill), create a caramelised topping on the brûlée.

To serve, place the ramekin in the middle of a plate and add a few slices of fruit (kiwi, strawberry) on top of the brûlée. Sprinkle with icing sugar, add a couple of shortbread biscuits and a pot of fruit compote and serve.

Make a good crème brûlée and people will show you a lot of respect!

Clafoutis Aux Fruits
Fruit and almond clafoutis

This sweet reminds me of going to my grandparents in the north of Paris. I used to pick the cherries and yellow and purple plums from their trees, and around 4 o'clock in the afternoon, my grandmother used to disappear into the kitchen and re-appear 30 minutes later with this great dish of hot flan. With all the lovely fruit on the top and 3 big spoons of ice cream – what a treat that was. Oh I do miss them.

This dessert is a light sweet flan, full of flavours of almond, vanilla and fruit. You can use all kinds of fruits, fresh, canned, pear, peach, apricot, cherry etc… I like to serve the clafoutis with a scoop of ice cream. The contrast of hot and cold is magic. This sweet should be cooked at the last minute and served straight away – so be aware, it will take a maximum of 15 minutes for them to be ready to serve.

Ingredients

Tin of peach halves or any fruit such as apricots, cherries or peaches

Clafoutis batter

5 small eggs

150g granulated sugar

75g self raising flour

70g ground almonds

200ml whipping cream

150ml milk

25ml dark rum

1 tsp vanilla essence

Icing sugar for dusting

Method

To prepare the batter, whisk the eggs in the bowl for 1 to 2 minutes until frothy. Whisk in the sugar, then add the flour and almonds and whisk for a further minute until well blended. Add the cream, milk, vanilla essence and rum and allow the mixture to rest for about 10 minutes.

Letting the batter rest allows the flour to relax, making for a more homogeneous batter.

In individual porcelain baking dishes or ramekins, place the fruit in a single layer. Carefully pour the batter over the fruit. Any excess batter can be kept in the fridge for a day or two.

Place the clafoutis in a preheated oven 180C/350F/Gas 4, and bake for about 10 to 13 minutes, until they become raised, golden and firm in the centre.

To serve, after taking them out of the oven, place them on a larger plate and serve straight away with a scoop of pistachio or vanilla ice cream and dust with icing sugar.

C'est délicieux, isn't it?

Les Desserts 73

Sticky Toffee Pudding
Sticky toffee pudding is delicious in French or English!

Well what can I say? It took me at least a life-time to find a recipe which Adele, my wife, gave me the magic word "oui!"

I tried and I tried and finally cracked it, when the sticky toffee pudding arrived on the La Boheme dessert menu. I like to cook my pudding in a large roasting tray, let it cool down and cut some nice big square portions; it's more for the presentation than anything else.

Ingredients

225g dried dates (chopped)

1 tsp bicarbonate soda

175ml boiling water

85g butter

140g brown sugar

2 eggs

2 tsp dark treacle

1 tsp vanilla extract

175g self raising flour

100ml milk

Toffee sauce

150g brown sugar

75g unsalted butter

250ml double cream

Method

Pour the boiling water into a saucepan and add the dates and dark treacle. Stir well, add the baking soda and bring to a simmer. Cook gently for 4 to 5 minutes, stirring often to prevent coating the bottom of the pan.

In a food mixer, cream together the soft butter, vanilla extract and brown sugar, and gradually add the eggs. Fold in the warm date mixture and the sieved flour, and add the milk to finish.

Line the bottom of the roasting tray with greaseproof paper, pour the mix into the tray and place greaseproof paper on top of the mixture. Bake in a preheated oven 170C/325F/Gas 3 for about 25 minutes and let it cool down before transferring onto a chopping board.

To make the sauce, gently melt the butter and sugar in a saucepan and when the mix starts to caramelise, gradually add the cream and stir well until the sauce becomes a nice brown colour – the sauce is then ready.

If you feel brave enough, you can cook the sticky toffee pudding 30 minutes before your guests arrive and keep it warm by placing foil over it. Or why not cook it in advance, let it cool down completely, cut into neat squares and warm the portions in the microwave for about 2 minutes each. That sounds much easier doesn't it?

To serve, place a warm piece of the pudding on a plate, pour some of the toffee sauce next to it, add a scoop of vanilla ice cream and dust with icing sugar.

Eat a lot of it and feel guilty because your diet has gone out of the window, but what a treat!

"Bread And Butter Pudding" De Maman
Mum's bread and butter pudding

I got this recipe idea from my mum. She used to make "pain perdue" every Wednesday after football – I think you call it French toast in England. Basically, eggy bread, but she used to top it with ice cream, vanilla sugar or chocolate powder. What a treat! I don't think Jamie Oliver would agree that this is a good diet for young boys though, what with all the sugar, bread, more sugar and sugary ice cream!

I once took this sweet off the menu, and after 3 days, nearly had a riot on my hands, so by popular demand, the bread and butter pudding is here to stay! I use brioche instead of bread as it makes it sweeter and smoother. You can also add rum or brandy into your mix to make it a bit more special. What a combination: hot bread and butter, creamy toffee sauce and vanilla ice cream.

This is one of the most popular desserts on the menu, and another winner at La Boheme. Life is sometimes so good!

Ingredients

300g brioche (approximately 1½ brioche loaf)

3 eggs

100g sultanas

1 tsp vanilla essence

300ml cream

150g milk

125g granulated sugar

Creamy caramel sauce

150g brown sugar

50g butter

300ml whipping cream

Method

To make the bread and butter mix, mix the eggs and sugar together. Add the milk, cream, vanilla essence, sultanas and break the brioche up into the mixture. Mix well until smooth. Leave the mixture for half an hour to soak.

Line 4 ramekins with clingfilm but leave plenty hanging over the edges.

Pour the mixture in to nearly fill to the top and wrap the top with the remaining clingfilm.

Cook in a bain-marie for 30 minutes, 180C/350F/Gas 4.

When cooked, the pudding should be firm on the top; if not, leave in the oven for a few more minutes.

Let the bread and butter pudding cool down and take out of the ramekins, keeping the clingfilm on.

To reheat, just warm in a microwave and then take the clingfilm off. I serve the bread and butter pudding with a caramel sauce.

Creamy caramel sauce

Gently heat the sugar and butter in a saucepan until the sugar becomes dark.

Add the cream, reduce to the right consistency and reserve until needed.

To serve, place a hot bread and butter pudding in the centre of a plate. Pour the caramel sauce on top and serve with a scoop of vanilla ice cream!

Don't forget to mention me and my restaurant when you take the applause from your guests.

Cheesecake Au Irish Crème Liqueur
Irish cream liqueur cheesecake

I got this great cheesecake recipe from Yannick, a French pastry chef, the best pastry chef I know. He makes some great desserts, but this cheesecake is something special. It is so light and the cream liqueur works so well. When you make it, you won't be disappointed.

Ingredients

150g amaretto biscuits or
130g digestive biscuits

40g unsalted butter

600ml double cream

250g cream cheese

70g caster sugar

150ml Irish cream liqueur

3 gelatine leaves

Method

For the base, place the amaretto biscuits in a food processor or mixer and blend to a crumb mixture.

Warm the butter in a microwave, add to the biscuits and mix well.

Tip the mix into a loose-bottomed cake tin or mould, press down to create an even layer and place in the fridge until needed.

For the topping, place the cream cheese, sugar and cream in a large mixing bowl and mix well with a hand mixer until all the ingredients are blended to create a soft peak.

Add the gelatine leaves to cold water (to clean them and to make them soft) and then, in a small saucepan, gently heat the cream liqueur, add the gelatine and stir until it is dissolved.

Leave the Irish cream to cool down for a few minutes and then fold into the cream mix.

Pour the cheesecake mix over the amaretto biscuit base in the cake tin and place in the fridge for 24 hours.

To serve, leave the cheesecake in the fridge until the last minute. To help remove it from the mould, boil some hot water, warm a knife, and gently go around the edge until all the edges are loose.

I like to serve it with a warm chocolate sauce! Tout simplement.

Parfait A La Façon Tiramisu
Perfect Tiramisu my way

What a great sweet to finish a great meal – guaranteed to be enjoyed by everybody. It is basically an ice cream with tiramisu flavours, served with a coffee and vanilla crème anglaise. I use Tia Maria, but you can also use Kalua. The chilled parfait (as it is called) will give you a lovely smooth texture and great flavours. Make the sweet at least a day in advance so it is nice and frozen when served.

Ingredients

8 eggs

200ml double cream

100g mascarpone

7oz caster sugar

5 tbsp Tia Maria

100g amaretto biscuits (roughly crushed)

Chocolate powder for decoration

1 tbsp coffee essence

Crème anglaise

200ml milk

4 egg yolks

50g caster sugar

1 vanilla pod (cut lengthways)

1 tbsp coffee essence

Method

To make the parfait, using an electric mixer, whisk the cream and mascarpone until it starts to thicken slightly - we call it soft peak stage. Pour it into a bowl and place it in the fridge until needed later.

Whisk the egg yolks in the electric mixer until they become pale and increase slightly in volume.

In a saucepan, bring the caster sugar and 3 tablespoons of water to the boil and reduce until the mix becomes syrupy (make sure the sugar stays white, if it turns brown, start again).

To check if the sugar is ready, have a glass of cold water next to you. Take a small amount of the hot sugar on a teaspoon and drop into the cold water. When the sugar cools down, you should be able to roll it into a tiny little ball with your fingers. If the hot sugar dissolves in the cold water, it is not ready.

You're now ready to pour the hot syrup into the egg yolk. Make sure the hand mixer is at full speed so the sugar will mix well, add the Tia Maria and whisk for a good 5 minutes.

Fold the semi whipped cream carefully into the egg yolk mix and add the coffee essence. Taste your mix and add more Tia Maria if required, then add the roughly crushed Amaretto biscuits

to the mix. Pour the parfait into a large terrine mould or individual Dariole moulds and place in the freezer immediately for 24 hours.

To make the crème anglaise, in a mixing bowl, mix the egg yolks and sugar together well. In a saucepan, slowly bring the milk and vanilla pod (cut in half lengthways) to the boil. When the milk is boiling, pour it into the egg mix and stir well. Pour all the mix back into the saucepan and over a very low heat, keep stirring (preferably with a little hand whisk) until the sauce starts to thicken.

To test if the sauce is ready, place the back of a tablespoon in the sauce – the sauce should completely coat the spoon.

Pass the sauce through a fine sieve and divide it into two. Leave one half as it is and add a few drops of coffee essence to the other half. This will give two different coloured sauces and two different flavours.

To serve, pour two good spoons of each sauce side by side onto a plate. Remove the parfait from the freezer and run the tip of a warm knife around the top. Place over the plate, turn over, and give a good tap to release from the mould. Dust the parfait with chocolate powder.

What can I say? Magnifique.

Tarte Aux Amandes Et Poires

Pear and almond tart

This is one of my favourite desserts. Pear and almond are a marriage made in heaven and the only downside is it's full of naughty calories! It's better to make the sweet pastry 24 hours in advance so the pastry can rest before rolling.

Ingredients

Sweet pastry

200g soft unsalted butter

200g caster sugar

500g plain flour

1 tsp vanilla essence

2 whole eggs

Almond filling

100g soft unsalted butter

100g caster sugar

100g ground almonds

2 whole eggs

1 tsp vanilla essence

1½ tsp almond essence

2 tbsp of rum

15g plain flour

6 pear halves (tinned)

Method

For the sweet pastry, place all the ingredients (not the eggs) in a food processor and mix well until it resembles breadcrumbs. Add the eggs and mix quickly (but not for too long). Place the pastry in the fridge to use later.

To make the almond filling, place all the ingredients in a food processor (but not the eggs or flour), mix well until the texture becomes creamy and smooth. Mix in the eggs and then the flour to finish.

Roll out the pastry and in lightly buttered, loose bottomed tart cases, gently place the rolled pastry inside each one. Cut off any excess pastry and place in the fridge for 2 hours to allow the pastry to rest. When ready, half fill the uncooked cases with the almond mix and place a half pear on top of the almond cream.

The pear can be cut into a fan shape and a few flaked almonds can be dropped on top of the tart if preferred.

Place them in a preheated oven 180C/350F/Gas 4, for 25 minutes. Leave them to cool down for about 10 to 15 minutes before taking them out of the tart mould.

To serve, while still slightly warm, place them on a plate with either a spoon of vanilla ice cream, double cream or clotted cream.

This is my mum's favourite and it could be yours!

Mousse Au Chocolat Blanc Et Frambroises

White chocolate mousse with raspberries

I always wanted to create a white chocolate dessert, but I didn't want to make it too sickly and this is the answer: white chocolate and fresh raspberries. You can't beat it!

Ingredients

200ml full cream milk

1 split vanilla pod

2 sheets gelatine

250g good quality white chocolate (chopped)

250ml cream

250g fresh raspberries

Raspberry coulis

2 punnets fresh raspberries

100g icing sugar

Method

Pour the milk into a saucepan, add the split vanilla pod and on a slow heat, allow them to infuse. Soften the gelatine in cold water.

Place the chopped white chocolate in a stainless steel bowl, pour half the hot milk over and whisk until the chocolate melts. Add the soft gelatine to the rest of the milk and once it has fully dissolved, add the warm liquid to the chocolate mixture. Mix well and leave to cool down for few minutes.

To make the raspberry coulis, simply place the fresh raspberries in a small bowl, add the icing sugar and blend with a hand blender. Pass through a fine sieve and set aside until needed.

To complete the dish, layer the fresh raspberries on the bottom of either ramekins, small moulds or a salad bowl. Pour the coulis on top until it covers the raspberries and place the mould in the freezer for about 13 minutes. This should be just long enough to help the coulis become slightly solid so that when you pour on the white chocolate, there will be two different coloured layers.

Lightly whip the cream and fold into the cooled chocolate. Pour the mousse into the moulds and place them in the fridge for 24 hours to set.

To serve, warm the bottom of the moulds in boiling water, gently turn out and decorate with fresh raspberries. If a large salad bowl has been used to prepare this dessert, it may be difficult to turn out, so will be best served direct from the bowl.

I like to serve this sweet with shortbread biscuits.

White chocolate heaven!

Tarte Au Chocolat Et Crème Fraîche
Chocolate tart with crème fraîche

This is one of my favourite sweets. In this recipe I use a mix of milk chocolate and dark chocolate to give me a very moist chocolate filling. In the past, I've had some chocolate tarts where the filling was too hard or chocolatey. This recipe will give you a light chocolate flan texture. It is also a nice and easy way of finishing a meal, you only need to slice it and serve it. I serve the tart with crème fraîche and a few strawberries or raspberries, but you can also serve with vanilla ice cream, clotted or double cream – the choice is yours. I strongly recommend you make the sweet pastry a day in advance, so it will be easier to roll out.

Ingredients

Sweet pastry

200g unsalted butter

500g plain flour

200g caster sugar

1 tsp vanilla essence

2 eggs

2 tsp water

Chocolate filling

200g dark chocolate

400g milk chocolate

2 eggs

600ml whipping cream

300ml milk

Method

Lightly butter or oil a 22cm/9 inch loose-bottomed fluted tart tin and reserve until needed.

In a food processor, place the flour, butter, caster sugar and vanilla essence and mix together thoroughly. Add the eggs, mix for about 1 minute, add the water and mix for another minute. Remove the dough, wrap in clingfilm and place in the fridge.

Roll out the pastry and carefully lift into the tart case, pressing gently to fit. Do not cut off any excess pastry hanging over the edge. Place a piece of baking paper into the tart case, fill with baking beans and chill in the fridge for 30 minutes. Meanwhile, preheat the oven to 180C/350F/Gas 4.

Place the pastry case in the oven and bake blind for about 15 minutes, then remove the paper and beans and bake for a further 5 minutes. Set aside for the filling.

To make the chocolate filling, in a large saucepan pour the cream, milk and chocolate, and gently warm until the chocolate has completely melted. Mix the egg with a hand whisk and add to the hot, but not boiling, creamy chocolate filling.

Preheat your oven to 200C/400F/Gas 6.

Place the tart base in the oven before pouring in the chocolate filling to help prevent the mixture from spilling out.

Once the filling has been poured into the base, reduce the oven heat to 150C/300F/Gas 2 and cook for about 30 minutes. The tart should be firm in the middle when cooked and the time could be extended depending on the oven temperature.

Allow the tart to cool down before cutting off the excess pastry, then remove from the tart case.

I would recommend you do this a few hours before the guests arrive so you will only need to cut the tart at the last moment.

To serve, cut the tart into 12 portions and place one portion on the side of the plate. Add a spoonful of crème fraîche and a few strawberries, then dust the tart with icing sugar.

Et voilà! This one is for all the chocolate lovers.

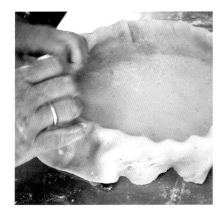

With grateful thanks to:

Amatos Dry Food
Mike
www.amatoproducts.co.uk

Arthur Gow - Accountants
Malcolm and Louise
Tel: 01477 571 392

Basefit Shopfitters
Russ
www.basefit-interiors.com

B&M Waste - Waste Disposal
www.bagnallandmorris.com

CIB Insurance
Dominic and Victoria
Tel: 0161-928 9675

Datum Contractors
Kieran
datum1@live.co.uk

Dave Repairs
Tel: 07767766052

Eagle Linen
Chris and Nicola
Tel: 01942 673 850

Elle Designs - Interior Designer
Toni
www.elledesign.co.uk

Essential Cuisine Stock
Neil
neil@essentialstockcuisine.com

Evergreens - Vegetables
Harry and John
Tel: 0161 775 0096

Funhouse Entertainers Balloons
Mannie
Tel: 07889707136

G P Broadhurst - Dairy
Ray
Tel: 01925 757 655

Gardener
Chris Payne

Glynn Brothers - Butchers
John and Tony
Tel: 0161 775 3103

Icelyn - Fridge Repairs
Jim
Tel: 0161 928 6851

Karl Welch Flowers
Tel: 01925 758 181

M&J Seafood
Joy
www.mjseafood.com

Matthew Clark - Drinks
www.matthewclark.co.uk

Maynards Stocktakers
Lynn
www.maynards.org.uk

Essential Cuisine Stock

88   La Boheme

Medway Oven Repair
Neil
Tel: 01942 203 628

Midlands Farm - Eggs
J Priestner
Tel: 0161 928 0654

Moss Farm - Potatoes
Mr and Mrs Clegg
Tel: 01925 752 434

Mouse House Print Shop
Dan and Sally
www.mousehouseprintshop.co.uk

Nisbets
Catering Equipment
www.nisbets.co.uk

Portland Wine
Ian and Jamie
www.portlandwine.co.uk

Powells Tea and Coffee
www.powellscoffee.co.uk

Safeguard - Kitchen Repairs
safeguardrefrigeration.co.uk

Shorrock Trichem - Cleaning
Joe
www.shorrocktrichem.com

Stephensons
Crockery and Glass
www.stephensons.com

Tattenhall Dairy - Ice Cream
www.cheshirefarmicecream.co.uk

Town & Country
Chocolates
www.tcfinefoods.co.uk

Vaclensa plc
Decarbonizer
www.vaclensa.com

Wellocks
Specialised Foods
www.wellocks.com

Woodwards Foodservice
Bread
www.woodward-foodservice.com

Window Cleaners
Kevin and Baz
Tel: 07967375128

Special Thanks To:
Paul Cons

Anne Perls

Jackson Hammond Design
Sheila Hammond
www.jacksonhammond.co.uk

Studio 6 Photography
Mark Duckett
www.studio6photo.co.uk

Triangle PR
Maha Hamer
www.trianglepr.co.uk

KITCHEN STAFF

Didier Gaulier
Alex Lush

Amy Tomkinson
Tom O'Hara
Lewis Grundy
Josh Fisher
John Boileau
Steve Potter
James Ballantyne
Chris McCaffrey
Dave Hannon
Alex Booth
Josh Hardman

And all our dedicated
current kitchen staff

RESTAURANT STAFF

Emmanuel Guichard
Jessica Smith

Andrea Smith
Jose Fernandez-Perez
Catrina Pennycook
Yvonne Dwyer
Dez Hayton
Charlotte Mills
Colette Alderson
Victoria Morton
Heather Hardman
Sarah Affi
Charlotte Nightingale
Andy Pemberton
Rachel Boardman
Megan Lever
Catherine Baxby
Louis Troalen
Naomi Fahey
Orlagh Fallon
Jenny Hossacks
Olivia Morley

And all our dedicated
current restaurant staff

OLD FAITHFULS

Alice Law
Charles Orr
Chris Maylor
Chris Hutchinson
Chris Ivison
Christophe La Garde
Christophe Montandrau
Claire Rooney
Colin Mutch
Dale Read
Emily Glancy
Georgie Marlow
Grace Law
Grace Mather
JB Montandrau
Joe Howard
Kevin Lynn
Larisa Smith
Libby Mather
Lisa Mather
Mark Smith

Martin Davies
Matt Nightingale
Melissa Yvonel
Mike Coles
Naomi Hannett
Nicola Britton
Rachel Maylor
Richard Hutchinson
Sam Howard
Sarah Latham
Sarah McDermott
Simon Griffiths
Simon Stewart
Sophie Griffiths
Stephanie Baille
Steve Moore
Sue Meade
Tim Scopes
Tim Orr
Yannick Megli

Come and see us again soon!